Trailblazers on the SEA

by Charis Mather

Minneapolis, Minnesota

Credits
Images are courtesy of Shutterstock.com. With thanks to GettyImages, ThinkstockPhoto, and iStockphoto. Throughout – GoodStudio, mhatzapa. Cover – Kate Demanovska, Kate Garyuk, TDubov. 6–7 – Ivan Marc, Sabelskaya. 8–9 – enciktat, NotionPic, vectornes. 10–11 – Naci Yavuz, VectorShow, Meilun. 12–13 – Sudowoodo, Cristoforo Dall'Acqua (WikiCommons). 14–15 – Macrovector, Augustus EARLE (WikiCommons). 16–17 – Olga Popova, Meilun. 18–19 – Wildlife Conservation Society (WikiCommons), funkyplayer, Ruslan__Grebeshkov. 20–21 – Bonnie L. Campbell (WikiCommons). 22–23 – Viacheslav Lopatin.

Bearport Publishing Company Product Development Team
President: Jen Jenson; Director of Product Development: Spencer Brinker; Managing Editor: Allison Juda; Associate Editor: Naomi Reich; Senior Designer: Colin O'Dea; Associate Designer: Elena Klinkner; Associate Designer: Kayla Eggert; Product Development Specialist: Anita Stasson

Library of Congress Cataloging-in-Publication Data is available at www.loc.gov or upon request from the publisher.

ISBN: 979-8-88509-955-4 (hardcover)
ISBN: 979-8-88822-130-3 (paperback)
ISBN: 979-8-88822-275-1 (ebook)

© 2024 BookLife Publishing
This edition is published by arrangement with BookLife Publishing.

North American adaptations © 2024 Bearport Publishing Company. All rights reserved. No part of this publication may be reproduced in whole or in part, stored in any retrieval system, or transmitted in any form or by any means, electronic, mechanical, photocopying, recording, or otherwise, without written permission from the publisher.

For more information, write to Bearport Publishing, 5357 Penn Avenue South, Minneapolis, MN 55419.

CONTENTS

Our Greatest Adventures by Sea....... 4
Leif Erikson................................. 6
Zheng He 8
Ferdinand Magellan 10
Jeanne Baret 12
Bungaree 14
Fabian Gottlieb von Bellingshausen .. 16
William Beebe 18
Dr. Sylvia Earle 20
Your Sea Adventure 22
Glossary 24
Index 24

OUR GREATEST ADVENTURES BY SEA

You have probably spent more time on land than on water. But most of the world is covered by water. Surprisingly, we have only **explored** some of it!

Lots of people have traveled on the seas. Some have even explored under the water. Let's learn more about these brave people!

Seas and oceans are both names for large bodies of salt water.

LEIF ERIKSON

Born: Around 970 Died: Around 1020

Leif Erikson was a Viking. He became famous when he took a ship to an unexplored land.

Leif Erikson was from Iceland.

Another Viking told Leif about a new land across the sea. Leif set sail and found what is now called North America. He named the place Vinland. But the name didn't stick.

Be Inspired!

Be curious about places you have never been to.

ZHENG HE

Born: 1371
Died: 1433

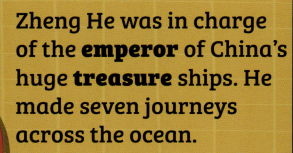

Zheng He was in charge of the **emperor** of China's huge **treasure** ships. He made seven journeys across the ocean.

Zheng He met many different people and even took some back to meet the emperor. Once, he brought the emperor a giraffe. Some people thought it was a magical animal!

Be Inspired! Try to meet people who live differently than you.

FERDINAND MAGELLAN

**Born: 1480
Died: 1521**

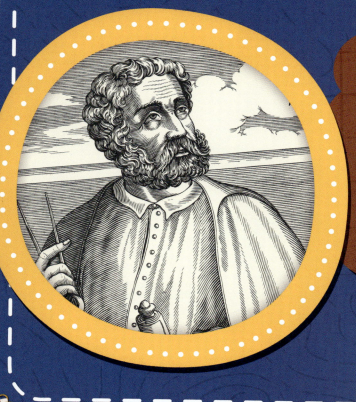

When Ferdinand Magellan was born, no one had traveled around the world. Ferdinand wanted to try. He took a new **route**.

Ferdinand Magellan was from Portugal.

Ferdinand's ships took a crew across the huge **Pacific Ocean**. They found land after 99 days at sea. But while they were sailing, they ran out of food. Ferdinand died but his **navigator**, Elcano, finished the journey.

Be Inspired!
Do not be afraid to have big goals.

JEANNE BARET

Born: 1740
Died: 1807

Jeanne Baret was the first woman to sail around the world. At the time, women were not allowed to sail on ships. But that did not stop her.

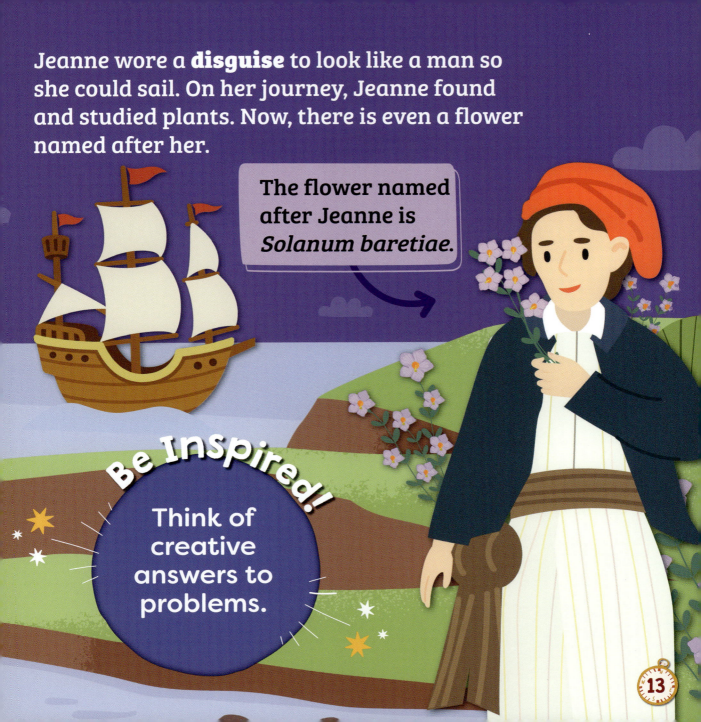

BUNGAREE

Born: Around 1775
Died: 1830

Bungaree was the first **Aboriginal** Australian to sail all the way around the country. He traveled with Captain Matthew Flinders.

FABIAN GOTTLIEB VON BELLINGSHAUSEN

Born: 1778
Died: 1852

Fabian Gottlieb von Bellingshausen was a Russian captain who sailed to Antarctica. He was the first person to see Antarctica's mainland.

Fabian's journey took more than two years. He met some **Maori** people on the way and bought food from them. Even though there were bad storms, Fabian was able to sail around Antarctica.

Be Inspired!

Do not give up, even if something seems impossible.

WILLIAM BEEBE

Born: 1877
Died: 1962

American **scientist** William Beebe studied life under the ocean. He was one of the inventors of the bathysphere.

The bathysphere was a metal ball that could take people under water. Although it was dangerous, the bathysphere helped William's team see new animals. The team set a record for the deepest dive.

Be Inspired!
Be brave and try new ideas.

DR. SYLVIA EARLE

Born: 1935

Dr. Sylvia Earle is an oceanographer. This type of scientist learns about the oceans and the things living in them.

She once walked around on the ocean floor. She wore a special deepwater suit. Sylvia set a record by going deeper than 1,250 feet (380 m).

Be Inspired!

Do not be afraid to go farther than anyone has before.

YOUR SEA ADVENTURE

People have been adventuring on the sea for hundreds of years. Some have traveled by ships to find new places. Others have gone underwater to learn about our world.

You can plan your own ocean adventure!

Use a finger to plan your route by sea on this map.

Who will you travel with?

What will you bring with you?

Will you travel in a boat or dive under the water?

23

GLOSSARY

Aboriginal the first people to ever live in Australia

disguise a costume that makes it hard to tell who a person is

emperor a person who rules over an area of land and its people

explored traveled to and found out about new places

Maori the people native to New Zealand

navigator a person who is trained to guide a ship from place to place

Pacific Ocean the ocean between North and South America and Asia

route the path to get from one place to another

scientist a person who studies nature and things in the world

treasure something valuable that is collected

INDEX

Aboriginal 14–15
Antarctica 16–17
bathysphere 18–19
flower 13
food 11, 17
land 4, 6–7, 11
record 19, 21
sail 7, 12–14, 16–17
scientist 18, 20
ship 6, 8, 11–12, 15, 22
treasure 8
Vikings 6–7